White House Correspondents Dinner, 2023: President Biden Fully Embraces The Dark Brandon Meme

By

Gregory D. Richardson

Copyright

Table of Contents

Chapter 1: The "Dark Brandon" Meme and the Rationale for the Biden Campaign's Adoption of It.

Initially, the growth of "Dark Brandon," Vice President Biden's hipper, more perceptive online persona, raised a lot of challenging concerns regarding memes and their historical context.

Who decides what a meme represents? Can a meme that originated in darkness, like the racist 4chan corners, possibly evolve to have lighter meanings? Do we have a duty to eliminate memes of questionable origins from our cultural lexicon, or would doing so just result in the total eradication of internet culture?

But because of how quickly and decisively the Dark Brandon meme gained popularity among Biden supporters, it has effectively come to represent not only Biden himself but also the internet's capacity to recover and save what was once lost.

The "Brandon" meme, which started as a humorous twist on an already hilarious meme from the right, has transformed into a triumphal hymn for the Biden campaign over the last year or two because Democrats, including various legislators and White House staff members, began using it. Recent site visitors to Biden's freshly announced 2024 campaign website noticed the site's

404 (page not found) landing page operating as a "Dark Brandon" Easter egg and directing users to a unique "Dark" campaign t-shirt with the Brandon picture.

Not bad for a meme that first appeared as "Let's Go Brandon," a right-wing rallying cry that was coded to stand in for "Fuck Joe Biden." Before the "Dark Brandon" variation took off, previous attempts to reclaim "Let's Go Brandon" for the left had failed miserably.

Dark Brandon frequently makes an appearance as a laser-eyed Joe Biden, usually in the form of an old-school lolcats picture macro, possibly with some allusion to some malarkey being defeated.

Late in the summer of 2022, the meme started to get viral and trend on Twitter. Right-wing commentators like Ben Shapiro made fun of it, while other commenters complained that the liberals had spoiled their joke.

However, despite the imagery's dubious provenance and potential for embarrassment, many Biden supporters enthusiastically adopted it and ran with it. The image went viral at a time when the real Joe Biden was enjoying a run of successful legislative initiatives. Because of Biden's accomplishments and the public's need for a new source of leftist inspiration, Dark Brandon became an unstoppable memetic hero.

This may all seem like simple, enjoyable superhero fun at first glance. The pleasant appeal conceals a far more murky past, however, as is the case with so much of the internet these days. Irony attached to these memes is often employed, particularly by the extreme right, to obfuscate and distort their fundamental purpose, which makes it unclear whose interests the memes are supporting. The internet, however, exists. Do we have any options for addressing that? Should we try at all?

Let's proceed with the analysis of a meme featuring an elderly man with Godzilla eyes.

Joe Biden is a well-known public person who is unassuming. It surprises me how memorable he is.

Since the "Deplorables" era of Trump memes from 2015–16, images created by his supporters have portrayed the former president as a testosterone-fueled Rambo-style warrior, intrepidly riding tanks or enormous bald eagles toward a hyperbolic victory over the libs, flags waving.

Regardless of their degree of internet fluency, far-right agitators have always benefited from this kind of imagery. This is because a large portion of their philosophy and approach include coded words, red herrings, and a grandiose aesthetic that blends well with the unreliable kind of comedy. Whether you read it humorously or not, it still works.

Joe Biden, in comparison, has had a more pliable reputation in online culture for a long time. The internet adored him as a lovable sidekick when he served as vice president during the Obama presidency. The Onion is renowned for popularizing a parody, souped-up version of Biden known as "Diamond Joe" — an everyman with a ponytail who enjoyed Dude Things like motorcycles, tinkering with his Trans Am, and temporarily cooling his heels in Mexico.

Although Biden's public persona in the Obama era was somewhere between a neighborly Dad and a drill tweet, during his election campaign, Biden's supporters didn't seem to be motivated to memefy him. On the other side, his adversaries quickly outdid them by labeling him "Creepy Uncle Joe." Although there is a whole industry dedicated to "Sexy Joe Biden," the meme never really returned in the post-Obama era. Even Saturday Night Live struggled to make a spoof of Biden that didn't fall victim to the perception of Biden's blandness.

A political meme culture that now more than ever depends on layers of irony doesn't readily lend itself to the folksy, homegrown Biden who shouts out "malarkey" and claims to have informed Vladimir Putin he has no soul. The longest-running representation of Biden in popular culture is of an elderly man savoring a vanilla ice cream cone, which is hardly an antithesis to the hyper-aggressive "America, fuck yeah!" sentiments of, say, the typical Trump meme or Trump's digital trading cards. It is everything that Trump and his memes are not, just like Biden himself.

The somewhat unassuming public image that increased Joe Biden's relatability with voters yet seemed to have worked to his advantage throughout the Biden administration. To restore his public image, Biden has committed to avoiding the spotlight and working mostly behind the scenes. Enter viral memes that transform him into his complete antitheses, such as a belligerent, red-eyed one-man army or supergenius. That internet culture would be weaponized in his favor came from the extreme right was probably inevitable.

"Dark Brandon" mixes two pro-Trump meme subgenres and makes an effort to spoof each of them. But things become very, very difficult from there.

The "Let's Go Brandon" meme started after a reporter misheard a crowd shout at the Talladega racetrack in October 2021. This mishearing may have been intentional. Brandon Brown, the race winner, was being interviewed by NBC's Kelli Stavast following his first career victory when screams of "Fuck Joe Biden!" erupted in between races. Stavast promptly created something which Trump-loving shitposters like most: a code for what they want to say in public but are unable to do so, disguised as something unimportant. The background noise was instantly translated into "Let's go, Brandon" by Stavast.

From then, the meme traveled what are now common paths into popular culture. Trumpists used it everywhere, even in Congress, and it was quickly devoured by conservative merch hawks looking to make a quick buck. Liberals attempted to turn it into a serious "Thank You, Brandon" meme, but it was a complete failure.

A linguist made a concerted effort to make the meme seem more significant than it was, like a win for the right and a deeper junction of linguistics and culture. It mostly followed a familiar pattern of back-and-forth efforts to free the meme from its initial satirical moorings, each of which only served to make it weaker. The "Let's Go Brandon" campaign is a sad echo of the Trump movement's early optimism, according to Forbes' Dani Di Placido in late 2021. However, this movement had degenerated into cringe-worthy bumper stickers and unimpressive bumper stickers.

However, as is always the case when discussing Trumpist politics, the actual harmful things it was (sometimes literally) adjacent to undermine the claim that none of this stuff is harmful:

Separate from "Let's Go Brandon," extreme-right memes had been shifting away from the original, testosterone-heavy

Trump memes and toward a harder aesthetic. A style of right-wing memery known as "Dark MAGA" (or "DarkMAGA") is more artistically nihilistic than even the standard sardonic Trumpist meme. It's kind of like a "gritty" DCU take on a far-right meme worldview that is now much more edgy and specifically geared at Nazis.

Dark MAGA memes often include a lot of neo-Nazi symbols as well as violent, white supremacist, and accelerationist ideologies. Consider swastika backdrops, pictures of Trump as a brutal dictator, and fascist language.

Combining these two right-wing clichés gave rise to the idea of "Dark Brandon," replete with grimdark Batman allusions.

That portion is really simple. However, there is no easy way to follow this meme's development or discover its original intent moving forward. Nobody is really clear how "Dark Brandon" got its start.

According to some reports, Dark Brandon started as a satirical far-right meme created by fervent conservatives who despise Biden and shaped him to fit their style. Others assert that it was made by "snarky leftists" who repurposed the Dark MAGA memes to ironically express how they felt about Biden.

Others assert that it was made by leftists who were parodying right-wing hypermasculine memes in an ironic attempt to mock Trump and his supporters. (One claim that the whole meme was created by Chinese propagandists temporarily gained traction owing to Yang Quan, a Chinese artist who created propaganda graphics portraying Biden as the Game of Thrones-style leader of an army of undead zombies on the Chinese social media platform Weibo.

The artwork gained popularity and entered the ranks of the Dark Biden memes after being decontextualized. There is no more proof that Chinese propaganda influenced the memes.)

You can probably already understand the difficulties that result from attempting to connect a style with neo-Nazi roots to a popular person whose edgiest memes entail eating ice cream. Democrats and Biden supporters, however, have continued to use the "Dark Brandon" idea despite this.

All of this is essentially a return volley. The Democrats who began to support "Dark Brandon" obviously intended to mimic the edgy "Dark MAGA" memes' appearance by fusing it with images of Biden as a tough-as-nails leader. MAGA fans reframed Trump's alleged fumbling ineptitude as a massive masquerade, a foil for the capable strongman that lay behind, using their outrageous memes.

Now, Biden's supporters are using the same strategy, portraying Biden as a macho, manly warrior who gets things done while masking his alleged fumbling ineptitude. Fair play, restitution, etc.

Since it gained widespread acceptance in the culture, however, Biden has adopted the meme in a way that suggests he is aware of both the meme's fundamental appeal and its usefulness to him as a means of rallying his supporters and reviving his once-tired public image.

White nationalist ideologies are widely adopted in internet culture. Should we take action in this case?

When we think about the meme's beginnings, even deeper questions emerge. Is it ever possible to truly reclaim memes for good if you're attempting to meme with visuals that may have formerly had a far more sinister context yet the original memes are still being used to spread hatred and violent ideology?

When he posted a "Dark Brandon" image that many conservatives claimed was ripping off the Nazi reichsadler, an eagle that was a component of the German coat of arms, White House deputy press secretary Andrew Bates came into that issue early on in the meme's ascent. Tobin Stone, who created the meme, said to the Daily Dot and the Washington Post that he had chosen a typical American eagle and that it was not based on Nazi iconography.

This situation highlights the difficulty of attempting to employ sarcastic memes with ambiguous and changing meanings for serious goals. Without the proper context, attempts to employ memes may often cause more confusion than they do clarity and purpose. And that depressing reality guides us toward a few more general conclusions about online culture in general.

The goals of extreme shitposters on opposing sides of the political spectrum eventually stop being opposed and begin to coincide. That moment may come when you're memeing the US president sticking a gun in an elderly woman's mouth, or it may have come earlier. It is difficult to discern between sardonic lefty shitposting and violent neo-Nazi shitposting on the internet, which is a reflection of the murky internet seas in which these kinds of memes develop. Additionally, it reflects the ambiguous ideological landscape where many formerly liberal public figures eventually begin to embrace and express extreme conservative viewpoints. A circle often represents the intersection of humorous hyperbolic trolling and attention-grabbing political ideas that lean toward violence and white supremacy.

It may have been detrimental at one point in the meme's development to attempt to distinguish between a "Dark Brandon" post that was used in an ironic way to support liberal causes and one that was used in an unironic way to support neo-Nazi causes. We had a meme that brought all of this baggage into the public eye and developed too quickly for it to be explained. But now that the Biden team has embraced it, it seems that, despite its sarcastic beginnings, it has become unmistakably a symbol of liberal ideas.

The fact that the meme's dark beginnings have been whitewashed further reflects the unsightly and little-acknowledged fact that, at this stage in the internet's development, a great deal of extreme far-right rhetoric and viewpoints have found their way into the mainstream. Due to the extreme far-right internet connection with gaming culture, geek culture, and several other cultural intersections, this occurs naturally and with ease. It's unlikely that the typical internet user who learns terms like "simp," "Chads and Beckys," "cuck," "normie," "wrongthink," or "redpilled" really knows their profoundly sexist and extreme roots, or cares that much if they do. If this lack of vigilance benefits anybody other than the garbage-eating deities of the internet, it usually serves the goals of the right-wing and trolls. However, it appears to have benefited Biden in this particular situation.

A pattern for using sarcastic online comedy in the service of progressive ideas and goals is something that "Dark Brandon" at least offers us. This is better than allowing internet Nazis to control our cultural lexicon and push us all closer to fascism. We may never be able to fully free this meme—and others that will undoubtedly follow—from the grip of the extreme right. It's less certain if using irony as a weapon to promote virtue and sound principles can last. But Democrats are at least making an effort by reclaiming "Dark Brandon." That's novel and cause for celebration; it's a victory for the internet. right now.

Chapter 2: President Biden's Zinger-Filled WHCA Dinner Speech Brings Dark Brandon to Life

President Biden arrived at the White House Correspondents' Dinner with jokes (and some serious statements), which irritated some reporters due to his absence from press conferences.

Joe Biden has been rather reticent to interact with journalists during his first two years in office. But on Saturday night, Biden and first lady Jill Biden attended the White House Correspondents' Association annual dinner with no signs of hostility.

The president seemed at ease as he sat at the head table on the dais with Vice President Harris and other dignitaries in the huge underground ballroom of the Washington Hilton. He was dressed neatly in a tuxedo. For the evening, journalists let go of their usual guarded reserve and extended a cordial welcome to the president of the country as is customary.

In his after-dinner speech, Biden threw in a few timely jabs. The president, who is 80 years old, acknowledged that people's apprehension over his impending reelection campaign was understandable. "I get that age is a completely reasonable issue," he remarked. The chairman of Fox Corporation, 92-year-old Rupert Murdoch, was then mentioned, and he said: "How could I dislike a guy who makes me look like Harry Styles?"

He also mentioned the $787.5 million defamation deal between Fox News and Dominion Voting Systems. He began by joking that "Fox News is owned by Dominion Voting Systems," adding that "[Fox staffers] are here because they couldn't say no to a free meal." He then said that "MSNBC is owned by NBCUniversal."

He contrasted sharply with his predecessor, who referred to the media as "the enemy of the people," by addressing the crowd that "the free press is a pillar, perhaps the pillar, of a free society — not the enemy."

The president also paid respect to two imprisoned journalists, Wall Street Journal reporter Evan Gershkovich and freelancer Austin Tice. Tice has been imprisoned in Syria for about 11 years now. The first American journalist detained in Russia since the Cold War, Gershkovich was detained by Russian officials last month on suspicion of espionage. "I'm working like hell to get them home," he said.

And Biden noted the presence of WNBA star Brittney Griner, who was exchanged for prisoners by his administration and freed by Russian authorities in December after being held captive for ten months.

Biden referred to an online joke that his campaign has recently embraced that claims the possibility of an evil presidential alter ego named "Dark Brandon" as he handed things off to Roy Wood Jr. of "The Daily Show," the night's featured comic.

He replied, "I'm gonna be fine with your jokes," before adding, "But I'm not sure about Dark Brandon."

Wood Jr. riffed on the two significant media firings that occurred this week: Tucker Carlson from Fox News and Don Lemon from CNN. The removal of Carlson from the airwaves, Wood argued, meant that "millions of Americans don't know why they hate you." Wood then turned to Biden.

He referred to Lemon as a "diva" who had degraded women on live, but he also said that CNN should have benefited from the media frenzy. He said, "That's a promotion at Fox News."

Although working journalists were, as usual, greatly outnumbered by publishers, advertiser-friends of publishers, dates of friends of publishers, and other people who have nothing to do with Washington or corresponding, there were even a few actual Washington correspondents.

In other words, the event mostly maintained its return to form following a few disappointing years that included cancellations due to the pandemic in 2020 and 2021 as well as President Donald Trump's boycott and criticism of the meal during his administration.

The opulent spring banquet included another first: a demonstration by around 100 climate activists in front of the hotel, calling on Biden to stop mining and drilling on public lands. The protest's reasoning seems to be that gathering a roomful of news media professionals is a very excellent venue to draw attention to your cause.

As a safety measure, Biden missed the gala's dinner section last year. He subsequently arrived to deliver the customary speech mocking himself and the media but left after about an hour. (Though Biden was unaffected, that meal did turn out to be a super- or at least a semi-spreader of the illness.)

The correspondents' organization was urged to submit a same-day negative test this year, but enforcement appeared to be lacking. Masks are also missing. Of the roughly 2,600 guests in the cramped, uncomfortable, and windowless ballroom, few were wearing.

The meal was one of the very few official interactions between Biden and members of the White House press during his administration, even though it was a social event with a focus on comity and humor.

According to the American Presidency Project at UC Santa Barbara, Biden has held only 20 press conferences during his first two years in office, which ranks third-lowest among presidents over the last 100 years.

Only Ronald Reagan and Richard M. Nixon had less (each had 14; Reagan's total was lowered due to his recuperation from an assassination attempt early in his first term, however). According to presidential expert Martha Kumar, Biden gives fewer interviews than any of his six most recent predecessors—just 58 in two years.

Biden's real working interactions with reporters have often been brief, hurried, and hectic, as before he entered the presidential helicopter or during photo ops in the Oval Office. Only Bill Clinton (394) had more of these contacts during his first two years than he did, according to Kumar.

The individuals sponsoring Biden's event on Saturday night have expressed dissatisfaction about the absence of more formal possibilities.

According to NPR reporter Tamara Keith, who is the head of the correspondents' group, "We're very frustrated," in an interview conducted a week before the event.

On Saturday night, Keith set it aside. She mentioned the arrest of Gershkovich in her speech. Deborah Tice, Austin Tice's mother, was also introduced by the speaker.

Arnold Schwarzenegger, a former California governor, and actor, opened the event with a recorded greeting in which he commended the press's efforts. "Without the press, I wouldn't be the Arnold you know. You are performing the will of the people, I tell myself. In contrast to his famed criticism, Trump referred to journalists as "the allies of the people."